ENCHANTING ORIGAMI

Magical Creature ORIGAMI

JOE FULLMAN

WINDMILL BOOKS

Published in 2021 by Windmill Books,
an Imprint of Rosen Publishing
29 East 21st Street, New York, NY 10010

Cataloging-in-Publication Data

Names: Fullman, Joe.
Title: Magical creature origami / Joe Fullman.
Description: New York : Windmill Books, 2021. | Series: Enchanting origami | Includes glossary and index.
Identifiers: ISBN 9781499485295 (pbk.) | ISBN 9781499485318 (library bound) | ISBN 9781499485301 (6 pack) | ISBN 9781499485325 (ebook)
Subjects: LCSH: Origami--Juvenile literature. | Animals, Mythical, in art--Juvenile literature.
Classification: LCC TT872.5 F85 2021 | DDC 736'.982--dc23

Manufactured in the United States of America

CPSIA Compliance Information: Batch BS20WM: For Further Information contact Rosen Publishing, New York, New York at 1-800-237-9932

Contents

Introduction

Let's explore the wonderful world of enchanted origami. In this book, you'll learn how to make unicorns big and small, as well as a fairy friend to join them in their enchanted forest.

In traditional origami, the models are usually made from a single sheet of folded paper with no cutting or gluing involved. We've broken the rules here and there to make our models as magical as possible.

Ask an adult to help with any projects that need scissors and glue. Otherwise, all you need to get started is a square of paper and your fingers. If you haven't made origami models before, try some of the easy projects first. Now, let's get ready for some fantastic folding!

Getting Started

The paper used in origami is thin but strong, so that it can be folded many times. You can use ordinary scrap paper, as long as it's not too thick.

A lot of these origami models are made with the same folds and basic starting designs, known as "bases." This introduction explains some of the ones that will appear most, so it's a good idea to master these before you start. When making the projects, follow the key to find out what the lines and arrows mean. And always crease well!

Key

- Valley fold
- Mountain fold
- Step fold
- Direction to move paper
- Push/flatten
- Rotate by x degrees
- Cut with scissors
- Glue
- Turn paper over

Basic Folds

Valley Fold

To make a valley fold, fold the edges of the paper toward you, so that the crease is pointing down, like a valley.

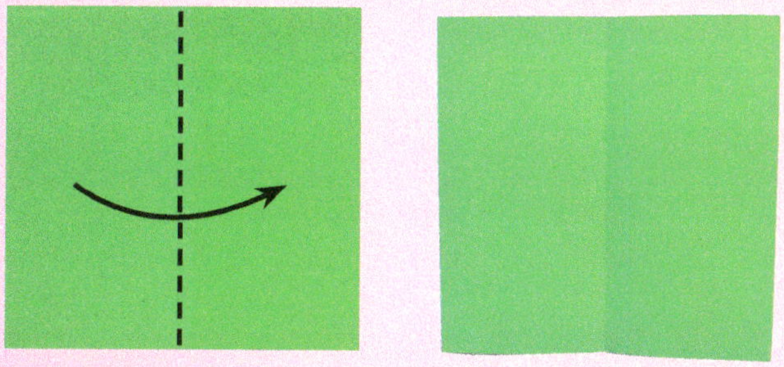

Mountain Fold

To make a mountain fold, fold the edges of the paper away from you, so that the crease is pointing up, like a mountain.

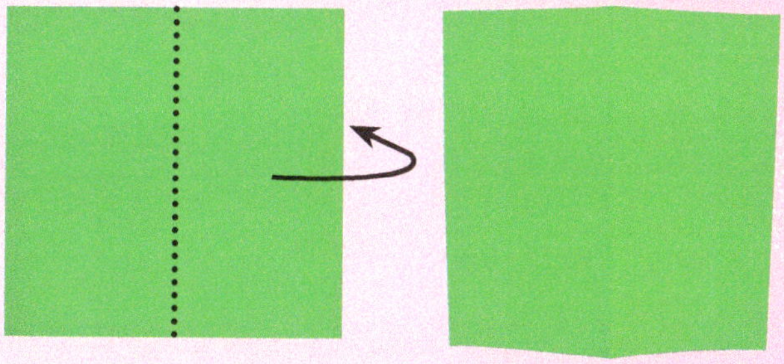

Step Fold

A step fold is used to make a step or zigzag in the paper.

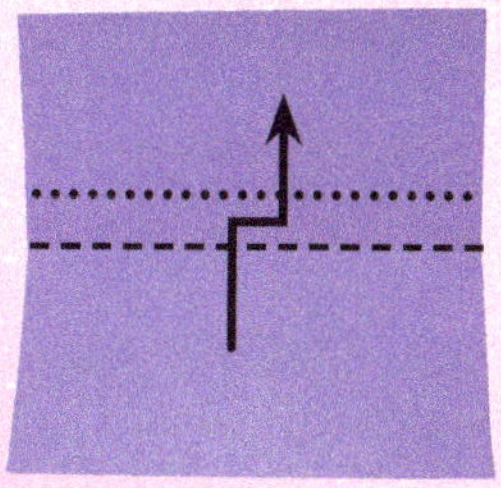

1 Valley fold the paper in half. Then make a mountain fold directly above the valley fold.

2 Push the mountain fold over the valley fold and press down flat.

3 You now have a step fold. You can also make it in reverse, with the mountain fold first.

Reverse Folds

Inside Reverse Fold

This is useful if you want to flatten part of an origami model. It's a good way to create legs and horns for your unicorns.

1

Fold a piece of paper diagonally in half, as shown. Make a valley fold on one point and crease.

2

It's important to make sure that the paper is creased well. Run your finger over the crease two or three times.

3

Unfold, and then turn the crease you've just made into a mountain fold. Unfold, and open up the corner slightly.

4

Open up the paper a little more and then tuck the tip of the point inside. Close the paper. This is the view from the underside of the paper.

5

Flatten the paper. You now have an inside reverse fold.

Outside Reverse Fold

This is great if you want to make part of your model stick out. It will come in handy for making heads and tails.

1

Fold a piece of paper diagonally in half, as shown. Make a valley fold on one point and crease.

2

It's important to make sure that the paper is creased well. Run your finger over the crease two or three times.

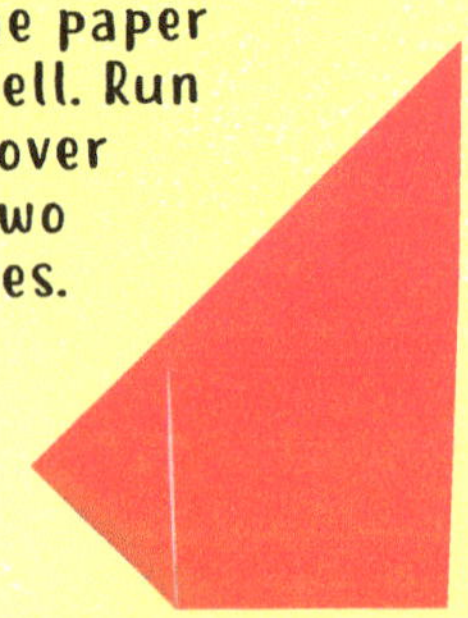

3

Unfold, and then turn the crease you've just made into a mountain fold. Unfold, and open up the corner slightly.

4

Open up the paper a little more and start to turn the corner inside out. Then close the paper when the fold begins to turn.

5

Flatten the paper. You now have an outside reverse fold.

Kite Base

1

Place your paper like this. Valley fold it in half from left to right.

2

Valley fold the left-hand point over to the middle crease.

3

Repeat step 2 on the other side.

4

You now have a kite base.

Magical Unicorn

Follow these instructions to make a special unicorn with a long horn filled with magic.

1

Start with a kite base (see page 7) like this. Fold the top-left and top-right edges over to the central crease.

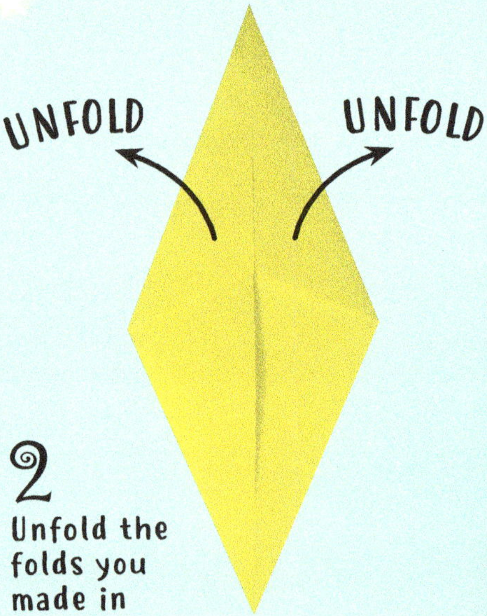

2

Unfold the folds you made in step 1.

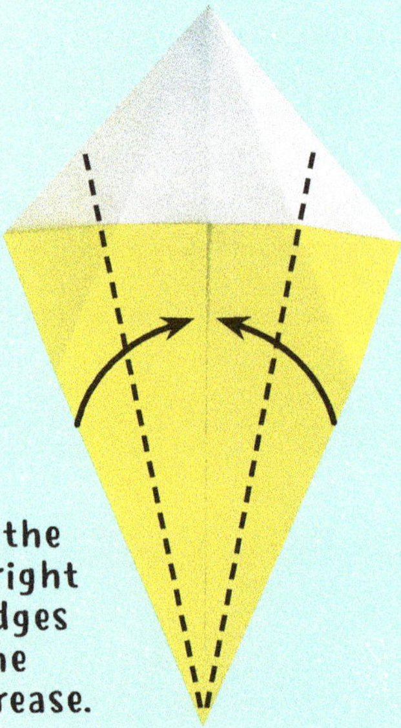

3

Now fold the left and right bottom edges over to the central crease.

4

Unfold the folds you made in step 3.

5

On the left-hand side, start folding the top left edge and the bottom left edge toward the central crease along the creases you made in step 1 and step 3. As you fold, pinch the paper on either side of the left-hand point.

Medium

6

The paper should start forming a point. Push it up and over toward the middle crease, then flatten it down.

7

Your paper should look like this. Repeat steps 5 and 6 on the right-hand side.

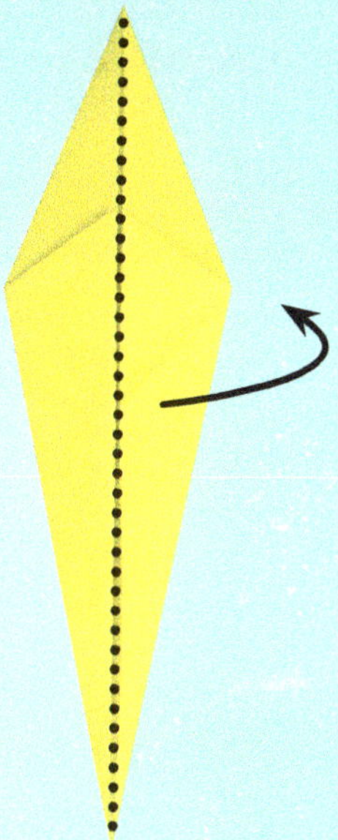

8

Mountain fold the paper in half from right to left.

9

Make a small valley fold in the upper flap, as shown.

10

Turn the paper over from right to left and repeat step 9 on that side. Then turn the paper over again from right to left, and rotate it to the right.

11

Fold the right-hand point up and to the left, as shown.

12

Fold it the other way, so it's also a mountain fold, then turn it into an inside reverse fold (see page 6).

13

Make a small mountain fold on the right. Fold it the other way, so it's also a valley fold, then turn it into an inside reverse fold.

14

Mountain fold the left-hand point up and to the right. Fold it the other way, so it's also a valley fold, then turn it into an inside reverse fold.

15

Flatten your paper down until it looks like the picture in step 16.

16

Mountain fold the top point down and to the left. Fold it the other way, so it's also a valley fold, then turn it into an inside reverse fold.

17

Flatten your paper down.

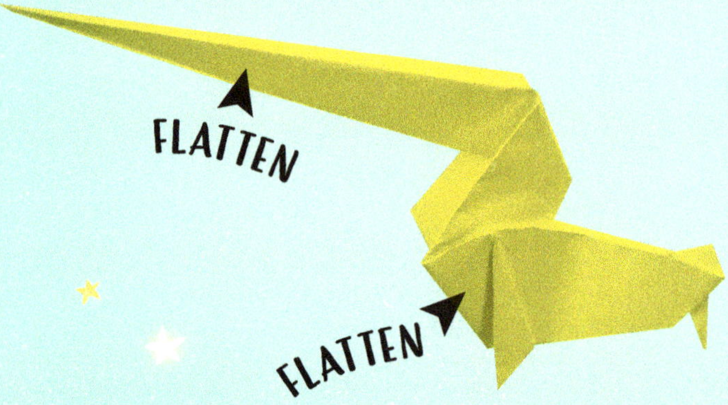

18

Mountain fold the left-hand point back to the right. Fold it the other way, so it's also a valley fold, then turn it into an inside reverse fold.

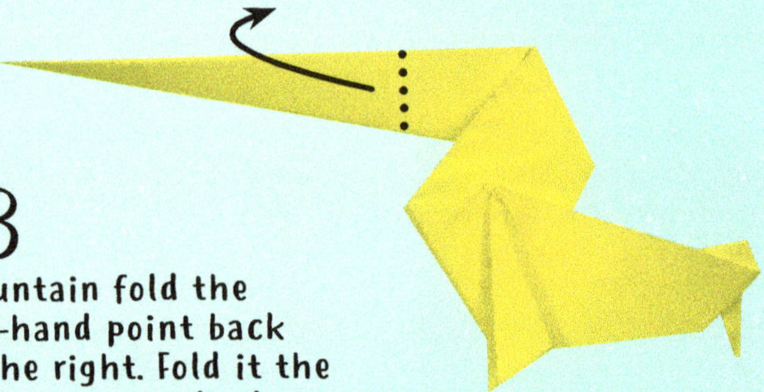

Medium

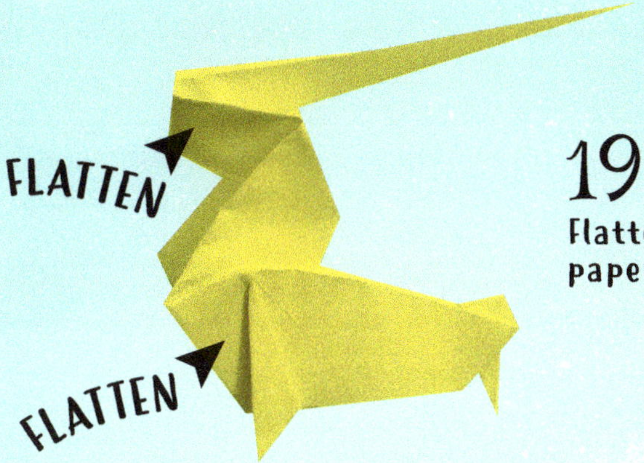

19

Flatten your paper down.

20

Pull the top right-hand point up and to the left slightly.

21

Mountain fold the right-hand point up and to the left so it sticks straight up. Fold it the other way, so it's also a valley fold, then turn it into an inside reverse fold.

22

Your paper should look like this. Flatten the paper down and make sure the horn is tucked inside the head.

23

Open up your model slightly at the bottom and your unicorn should be able to stand up.

24

Give your unicorn a happy expression—it's ready to start playing with its friends.

Fairy Friend

Unicorns aren't the only magical creatures in the forest. Here's how to make a fabulous fairy friend to flutter around with your unicorns.

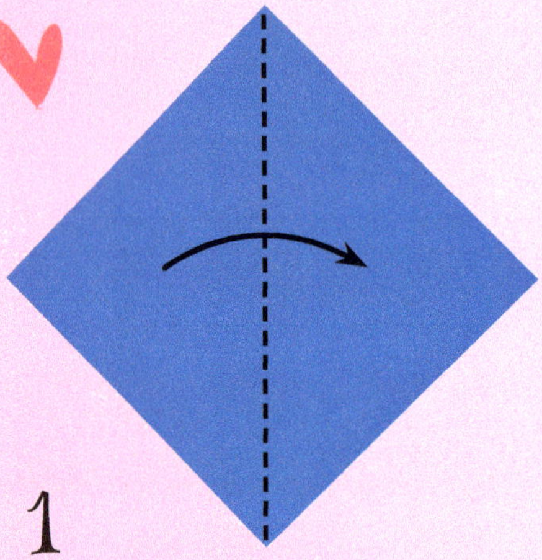

1

Start with your paper like this, white side down, with a corner facing you. Valley fold it in half from left to right, then unfold.

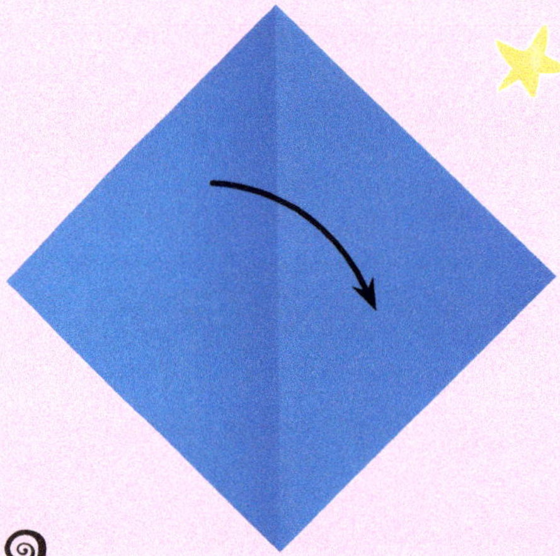

2

Valley fold the top-left edge over to the bottom right edge, but don't crease.

3

Press down to make a small crease on the top edge of the paper in the position shown. Then unfold.

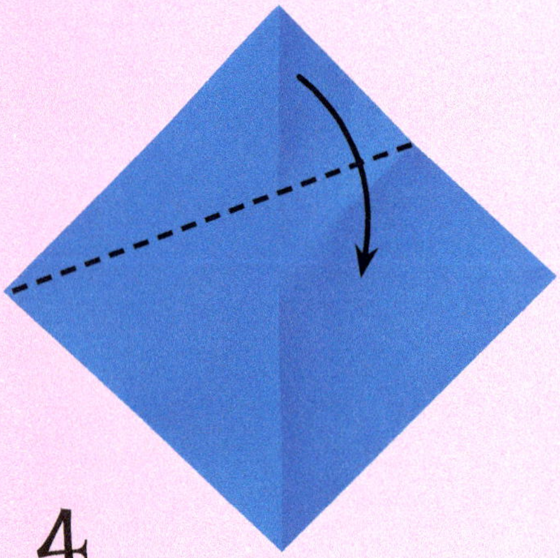

4

Make a valley fold between the small crease you made in step 3 and the left corner.

5

Unfold the fold you made in step 4.

6

Valley fold the top corner so it touches the point where the crease you made in step 1 and the crease you made in step 4 meet.

Hard

7
Unfold the fold you made in step 6.

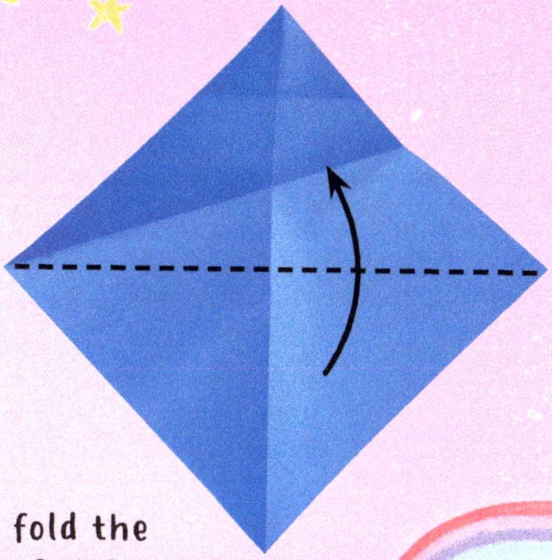

8
Valley fold the bottom corner up to the top.

9
Your paper should look like this. Turn it over from left to right.

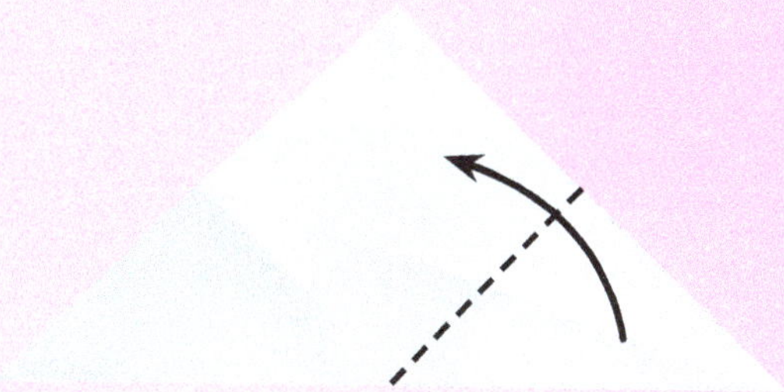

10
Valley fold the right-hand point up to the top point.

11
Repeat step 10 on the left-hand side.

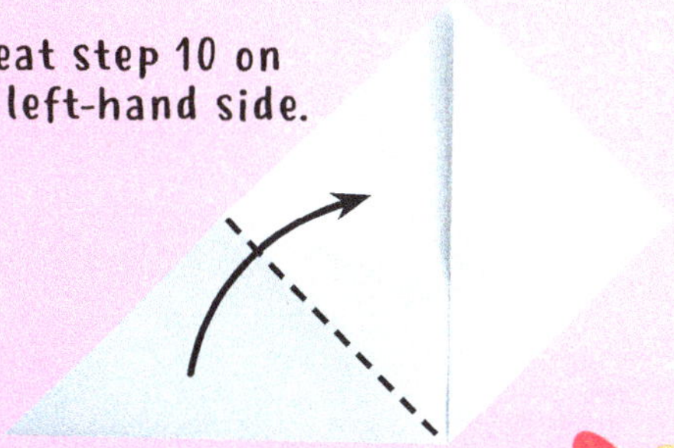

12
Turn your paper over from left to right.

13
Valley fold the top point of the upper layer down to the bottom.

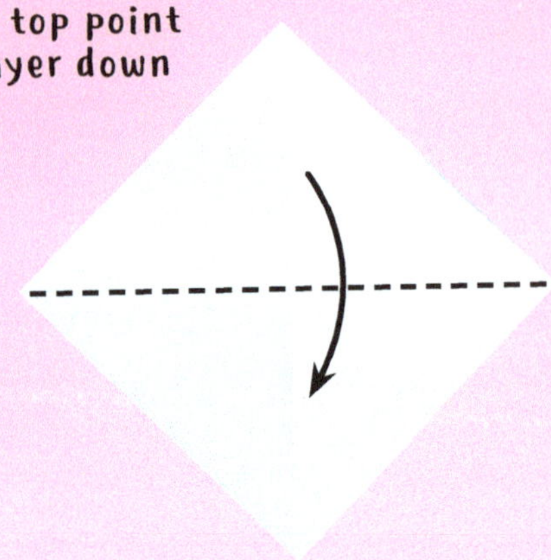

14
Fold over the top point of the next layer along the crease line you made in step 6.

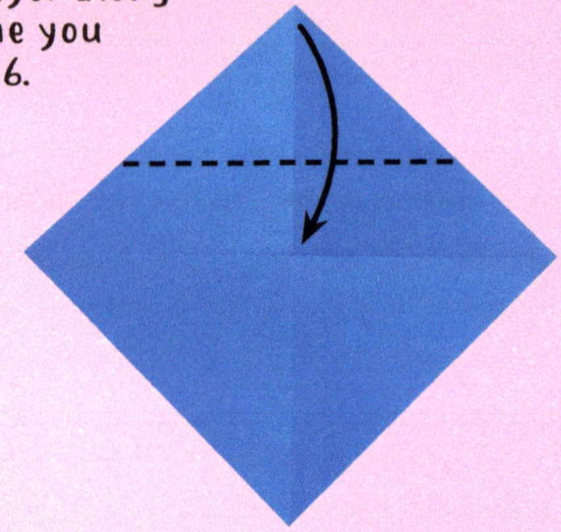

15
Turn your paper over from left to right.

16
Unfold the folds you made in steps 10 and 11.

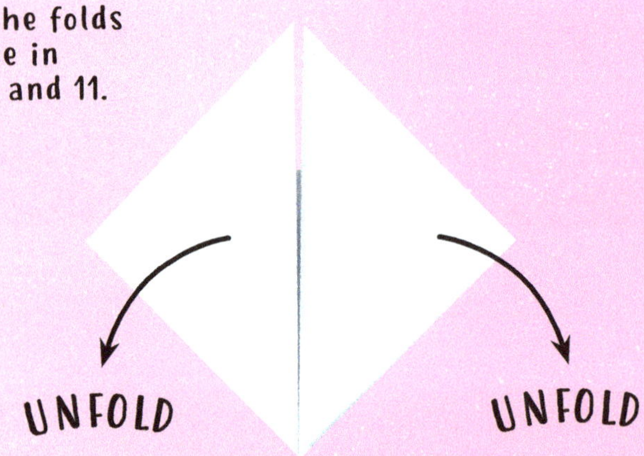

17
Make a diagonal valley fold on the right-hand side. The top-right point should touch the central crease.

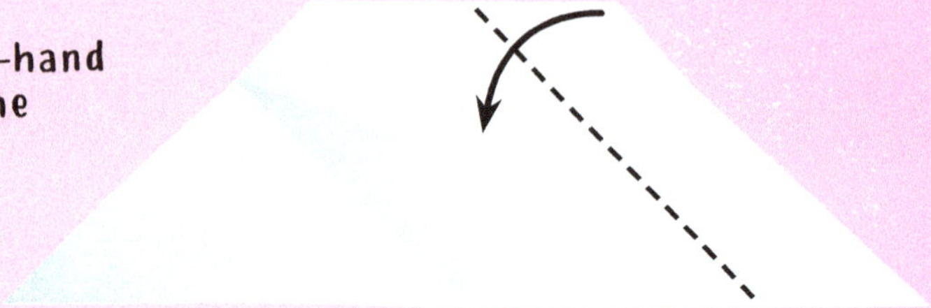

18
Your paper should look like this with a diagonal flap on the right-hand side with a white triangle at the top. Lift the white triangle a little so you can make another diagonal valley fold in the flap by turning the paper underneath the white triangle and pressing down (see image for step 19).

Hard

19

Keep the white triangle in position, and fold the flap under it over to the central crease. Flatten the paper down.

20

Your paper should look like this. Carefully unfold the folds you made in steps 17 to 19.

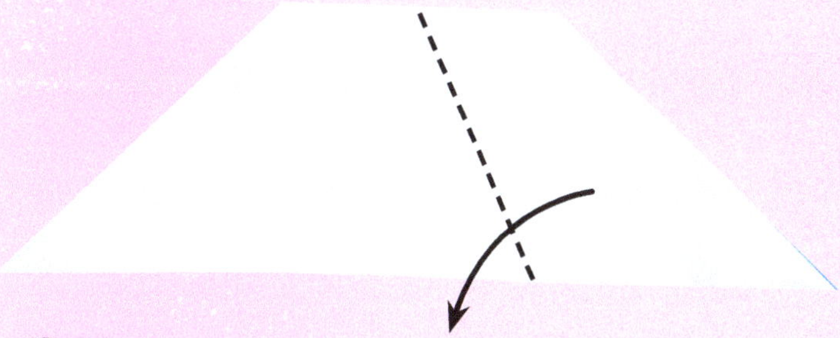

21

Make another diagonal fold on the right-hand side, using the lower crease line you made in step 19.

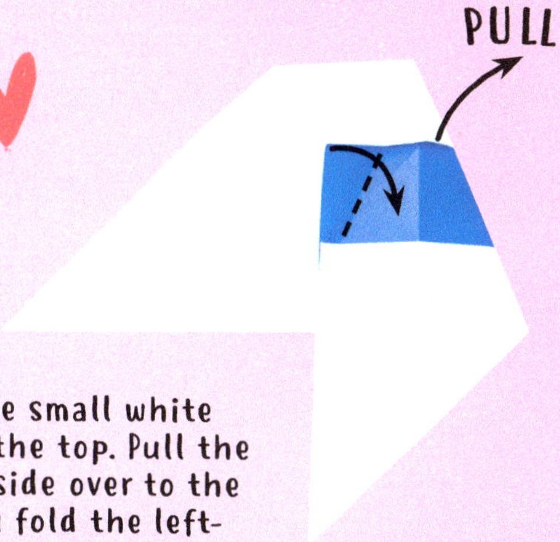

22

Open out the small white triangle at the top. Pull the right-hand side over to the right as you fold the left-hand side over the upper fold you made in step 19. Flatten the paper down.

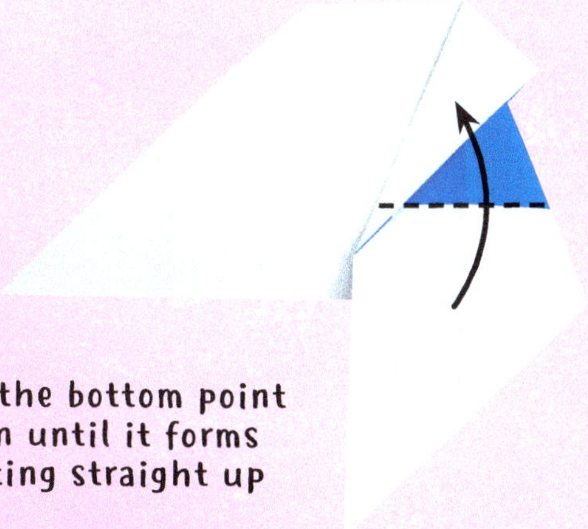

23

Valley fold the bottom point up as shown until it forms a flap pointing straight up toward you.

24

Continue lifting the bottom point toward the top. As you do, the right-hand point should start coming over to the left. Flatten it down over the other point.

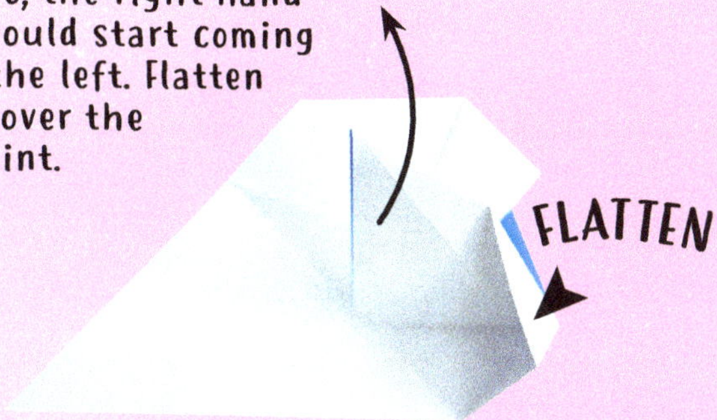

25
Valley fold the top point over to the right until it begins to form a semispherical shape.

26
Flatten the paper down along the line shown.

27
Make a small valley fold on the right-hand side, as shown.

28
Your paper should look like this.
Repeat steps 17 to 27 on the left-hand side.

29
Turn your paper over from left to right.

30
Make a small mountain fold in the top point.

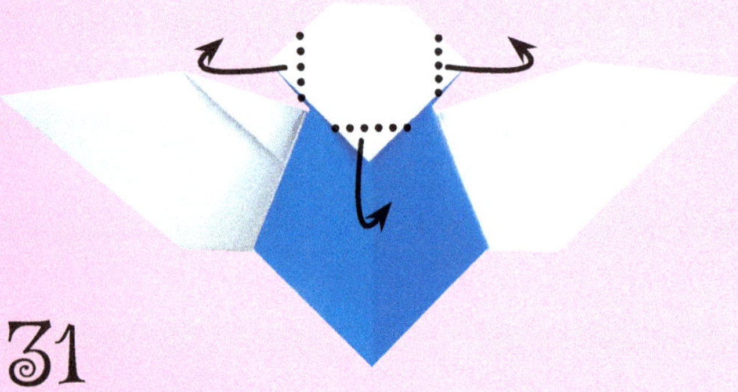

31
Make three more small mountain folds, as shown, to form the face.

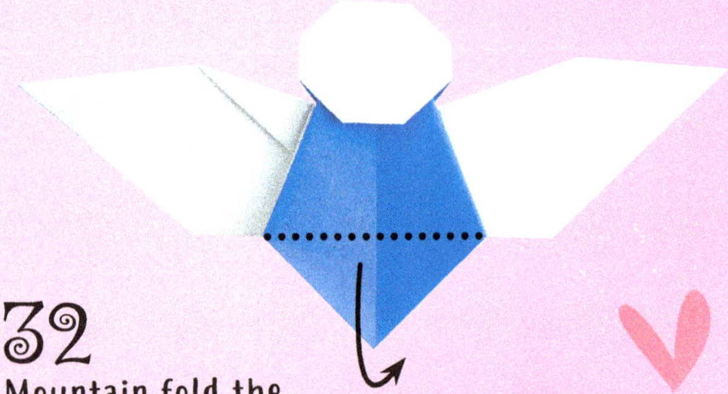

32
Mountain fold the bottom point of the upper layer and tuck it in.

Hard

33
Valley fold the bottom point that remains and tuck that in too.

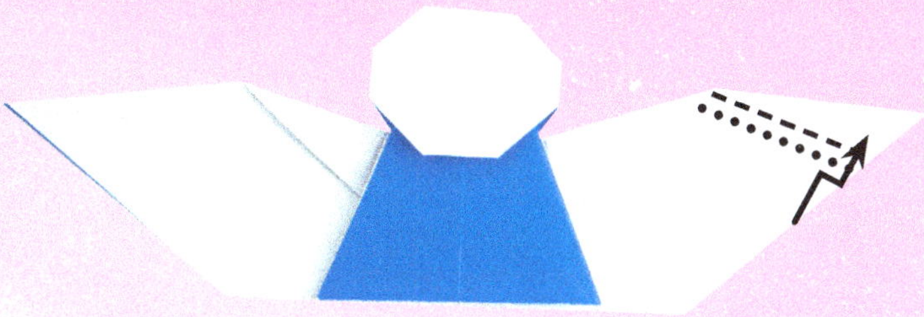

34
Make a step fold in the right-hand wing, as shown (see page 5).

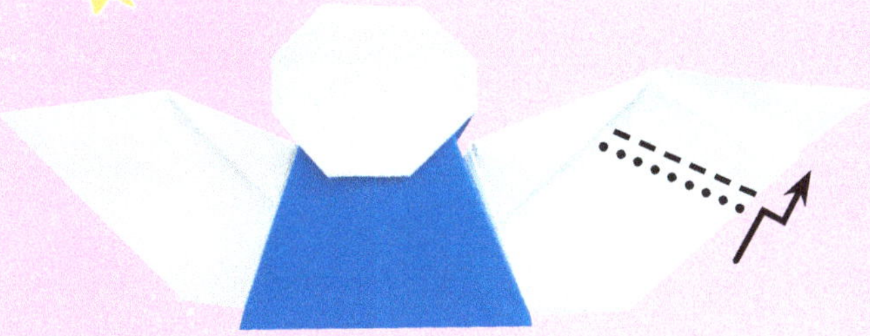

35
Make another step fold slightly farther along. Make sure the fold goes under the triangle at the top of the wing.

36
Make a third step fold to complete the wing.

37
Your paper should look like this. Repeat steps 34 to 36 on the left-hand side.

38
Give your fairy a happy expression. It's ready to play with the unicorns!

Little Unicorn

This cute unicorn is ready to join its friends in a magical forest. Why not make it a few brothers and sisters, too, using different types of paper?

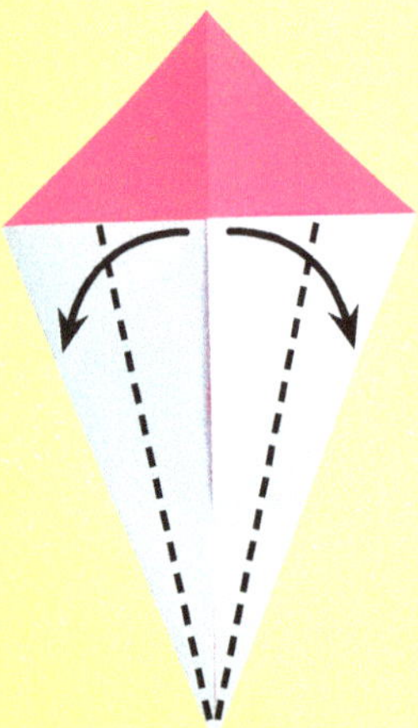

1
Make a kite base (see page 7), but start with the white side facing down so your paper ends up looking like this. Make two valley folds in the upper layer on both sides.

2
Turn your paper over from left to right.

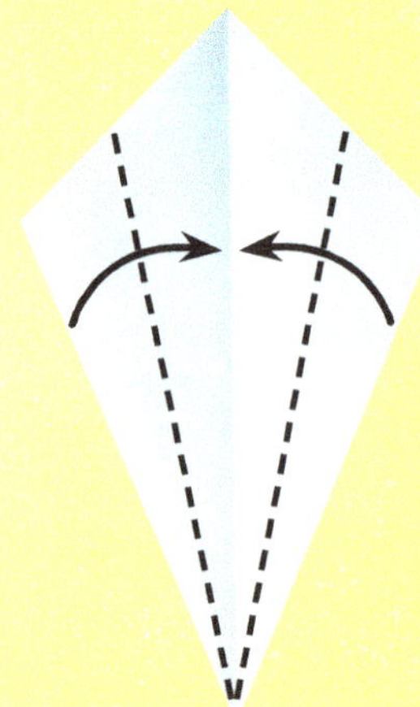

3
Make valley folds on either side, as shown, so that the edges line up with the central crease. Be sure to fold all layers.

4
Open up the upper left-hand flap and pull its top right point down so it begins to form a triangle shape.

5
Your paper should look like this. Keep the point in line with the central crease and flatten the triangle shape down.

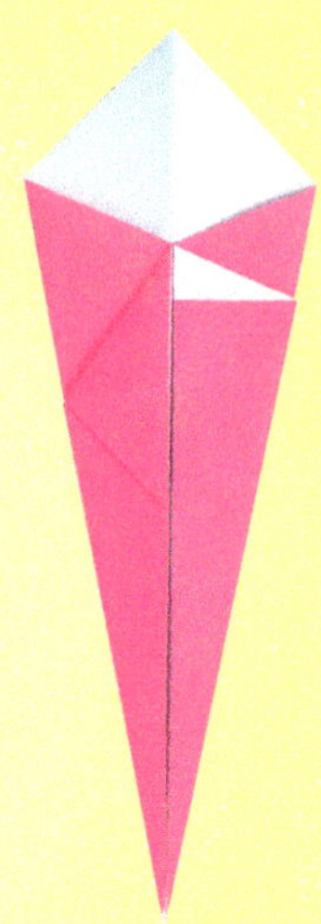

6
Repeat steps 4 and 5 on the right-hand side.

Hard

7

Valley fold the top left-hand edge over to the central crease.

8

Repeat step 7 on the right-hand side.

9

Open out the folds you made in steps 7 and 8.

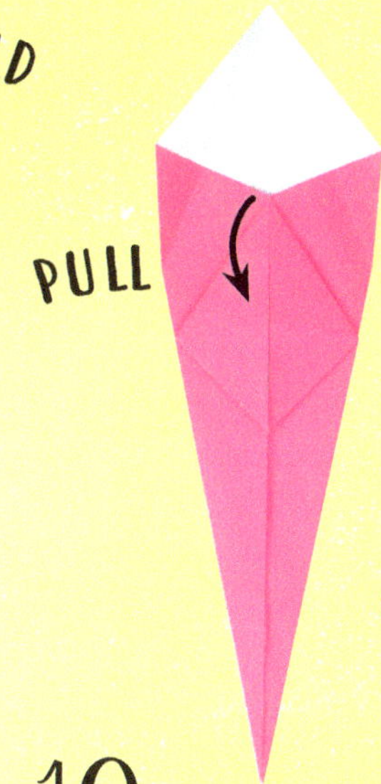

10

Open out the top left flap and, as with step 4, pull its top right point down so it begins to form a triangle shape.

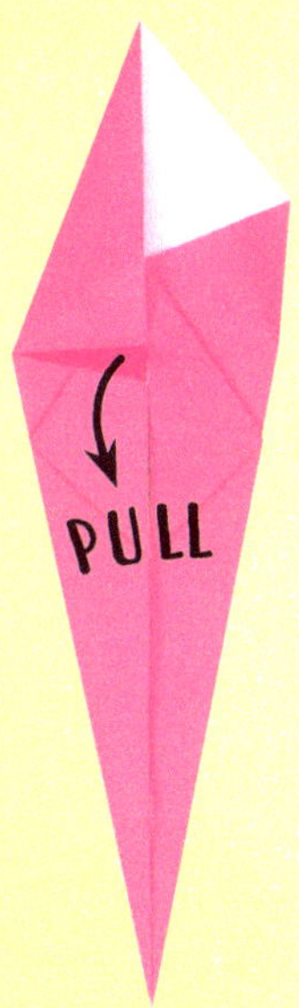

11

Keep pulling the point down in line with the central crease so the triangle shape goes over the flap you made in steps 4 and 5.

12

Repeat steps 10 and 11 on the right-hand side.

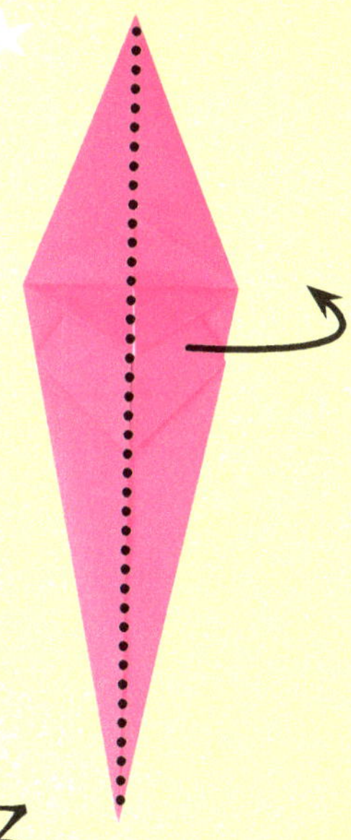

13

Mountain fold the paper in half from right to left.

14

Open out the top left-hand side of the paper above the left-hand point of the triangle-shaped flaps you made in steps 4 to 6. Rotate the open side toward you.

15

Pinch the top of the paper closed and open the paper out wide on either side of the triangle-shaped flaps.

16

Push each side down and around the triangle-shaped flaps at an angle. Flatten the paper down and rotate it clockwise so it lies flat.

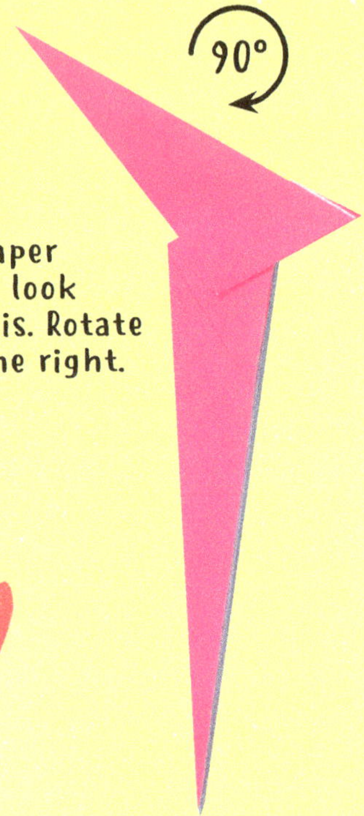

17

Your paper should look like this. Rotate it to the right.

18

Make a mountain fold as shown—note that the fold goes in between the two small triangle flaps you made in steps 4 to 6. Fold it the other way, so it's also a valley fold, then turn it into an inside reverse fold (see page 6).

19

Flatten your paper down.

20

Make a mountain fold as shown on the left-hand point. Fold it the other way, so it's also a valley fold, then turn it into an inside reverse fold.

21

Flatten your paper down.

Hard

22
Valley fold the top right point down and to the left at an angle, as shown.

23
Fold it the other way, so it's also a mountain fold, then unfold.

24
Open up the right-hand flap on the left side and push it down to the left so it forms a flat kite shape.

25
Make a valley fold over to the right at the widest point of the kite shape.

26
Push together the sides of the flat triangle shape you made in step 25. This should create a valley fold along its length. Flatten it down.

27
Your paper should look like this. Make a small mountain fold in the upper layer of the new right-hand point, as shown. Turn your paper over from left to right.

28
Repeat step 27 on this side, then turn the paper over again.

29
Make a valley fold in the right-hand point.

30
Fold it the other way, so it's also a mountain fold, then turn it into an outside reverse fold (see page 6).

31
Make another small valley fold closer to the end of the point.

32
Fold it the other way, so it's also a mountain fold, then turn this into an outside reverse fold too.

33
Open out the left-hand point. This will form the head, while the vertical piece in the middle will be the neck .

34
With the left-hand point opened at the top, push one side around the back of the neck and the other side around the front, as shown, so the point raises up.

Hard

35

Make a mountain fold in the left-hand point, as shown.

36

Make a mountain fold as shown, so the point sticks straight up.

37

This is what your paper should look like from behind.

38

Unfold the folds you made in steps 35 and 36, and fold them the other way, so they're also valley folds. Then turn them into two inside reverse folds, one inside the other to form the head and horn.

39

Make sure the horn is tucked into the head.

40

Your little unicorn is ready for its first gallop. Add some sparkly patterns!

Glossary

CREASE A line made by a fold.

DIAGONAL A line in a sloping direction, from one corner to another.

KITE BASE A starting shape that looks like a kite.

MOUNTAIN FOLD A fold where the crease points up, like a mountain.

STEP FOLD A fold that creates a zigzag, or step, in the paper.

VALLEY FOLD A fold where the crease points away from you, like a valley.

Further Information

James, Elizabeth. *Easy Origami for Children.* Twickenham, UK: Kyle Craig Publishing, 2017.

Montroll, John. *Dragons and Other Fantastic Creatures in Origami.* Mineola, NY: Dover Publications, 2014.

Stephen, Ella. *Origami for Kids.* Independently published, 2019.

Top That Publishing. *Fold Your Own Fantastic Fairytale Unicorns.* Woodbridge, UK: Top That Publishing, 2019.

Index